D1506143

THE LEGENDARY WILD WEST

A SOURCEBOOK ON THE AMERICAN WEST

THE LEGENDARY WILD WEST

A SOURCEBOOK ON THE AMERICAN WEST

Edited by Carter Smith

AMERICAN ALBUMS FROM THE COLLECTIONS OF
THE LIBRARY OF CONGRESS

THE MILLBROOK PRESS, *Brookfield, Connecticut*

Cover: "Custer's Last Charge." Lithograph by Seifert Gugler & Co., 1876, based on a drawing by Feodor Fuchs.

Title Page: "Tower Falls and Sulphur Mountain, Yellowstone." Chromolithograph by Prang & Company, based on a painting by Thomas Moran, 1874.

Contents Page: "The Great Train Robbery." Movie Poster, 1911.

Back Cover: "American Frontier Life: The Hunter's Stratagem." Lithograph by Currier & Ives, 1862, based on a painting by Arthur F. Tait.

Library of Congress Cataloging-in-Publication Data

The Legendary Wild West : a sourcebook on the American West /
    edited by Carter Smith.
        p.   cm. -- (American albums from the collections of the
    Library of Congress)
        Includes bibliographical references and index.
        Summary: Describes and illustrates the American West from
    1775 to 1912 through a variety of images created during that
    period.
        ISBN 1-56294-133-X (lib. bdg.)   ISBN 0-7613-0153-4 (pbk.)
        1. United States--Territorial Expansion--Sources--Juvenile
    literature. 2. West (U.S.)--History--Sources--Juvenile literature.
    3. Frontier and pioneer life--West (U.S.)--Sources--Juvenile
    literature. 4. West (U.S,) in literature--Juvenile literature. 5.
    West (U.S.) in art--Juvenile literature. [1. West (U.S.)--History--
    Sources. 2. Frontier and pioneer life--West (U.S.)--Sources.] I.
    Smith, C. Carter. II. Series.
    E179.5.L38 1992
    978--dc20   91-31126
                                                          CIP
                                                           AC

 Created in association with Media Projects Incorporated

C. Carter Smith, *Executive Editor*
Lelia Wardwell, *Managing Editor*
Elizabeth Prince, *Manuscript Editor*
Kevin Kelly, *Principal Writer*
Charles A. Wills, *Consulting Editor*
Kimberly Horstman, *Researcher*
Lydia Link, *Designer*
Athena Angelos, *Photo Researcher*

The consultation of Bernard F. Reilly, Jr., Head Curator of the
Prints and Photographs Division of the Library of Congress, is
gratefully acknowledged.

Contents

Keokuk, chief of the Sauk and Fox tribes, was painted by Charles Bird King in 1837, when the chief led his nation's largest delegation to Washington. A distinguished warrior, chief, and diplomat, Keokuk came to Washington to debate with government officials over the establishment of territorial claims on the lands of the Sauk and Fox nations in what is now Iowa. Known for his oratory skills, Keokuk was praised for his eloquent defense of Indian lands. He died in Kansas in 1848.

Introduction

THE LEGENDARY WILD WEST is one of the volumes in a series published by The Millbrook Press titled AMERICAN ALBUMS FROM THE COLLECTIONS OF THE LIBRARY OF CONGRESS and one of six books in the series subtitled SOURCEBOOKS ON THE AMERICAN WEST. This series treats the history of the West from pioneer days to the early twentieth century.

The editors' goal for the series is to make available to the student many of the original visual documents of the American past that are preserved in the Library of Congress. Featured prominently in THE LEGENDARY WILD WEST are the rich holdings of the Prints and Photographs Division, and many of the illustrated books, almanacs, and periodicals found in the Library's Rare Book and Special Collections Division.

The images from these sources reflect the persistent ambiguity of American attitudes toward the West. On the one hand, they show a scientific curiosity about this enormous expanse of territory. On the other, they indicate the tendency to create an imaginary and heroic world. Accordingly, the illustrations shown here run the full gamut of relative objectivity, veering back and forth between factuality and fantasy from the beginning of the century to its close.

Naturalists were responsible for thousands of images of the West. Among them were Titian Peale's drawings from the 1819 and 1823 expeditions to the West led by Major Stephen Long, John James Audubon's engravings of the birds and quadrupeds of North America, and George Catlin's Indian Gallery and the corresponding portfolio of North American Indians. These endeavors, undertaken in the spirit of scientific inquiry, found a ready popular audience in the East and in Europe.

The woodcut illustrations of the Lewis and Clark explorations, published in Patrick Gass's journal of the 1805-07 expedition, have less scientific than amusement value in their primitive but matter-of-fact reporting of such incidents as capsizing boats and encounters with hostile bears.

The Crockett almanacs, which originated in Tennessee in the late 1830s and were widely copied thereafter, regaled antebellum Easterners with the preposterous backwoods exploits of Davy Crockett. What these did for the real David S. Crockett, the dime novel did for the historical cowboy later in the century. From these and from the magazine illustrations of the prolific Frederic Remington emerged the romantic myth of the cowboy and the Wild West. In these still pictures were created the legends which became a staple of American cinema in the twentieth century.

In terms of the Western landscape itself, Thomas Moran's paintings of Yellowstone, the Grand Canyon, and other natural features were unrestrainedly theatrical and romanticized. To Moran's rhapsodic visions, Carleton Watkin's photographs of Western scenery offer a sober antidote, but one which is no less enchanting and exotic.

The works reproduced comprise only a sampling of the rich record of Western life preserved by the Library of Congress in its role as the nation's library.

BERNARD F. REILLY, JR.

In a woodcut from Davy Crockett's 1838 Almanack *(left), two rugged men save a woman from a snake and a ferocious mountain lion—the promise of adventures such as this lured many Americans out West.*

From the time Europeans began exploring the frontier in the mid-seventeenth century, the American West had been considered a dangerous but exciting land. It offered endless opportunities for adventure and success to those bold enough to venture into the wilderness. Explorers, such as the legendary Daniel Boone, were heading west and returning with marvelous stories of the rich and rugged land that lay beyond the mountains.

Stories of the strange, new land that lay west of the Mississippi River prompted much speculation. Almost immediately, the federal government began exploring and surveying the land between the Mississippi River and the Rocky Mountains.

Visual accounts of these trips were often provided by artists who joined the explorers. A great deal of what we know of the early westward movement and Indian life comes from the paintings and sketches of Carl Bodmer, Titian Peale, Seth Eastman, and George Catlin. Their work generated excitement about the frontier and helped create a romantic ideal of the West.

By mid-century, Eastern newspapers and magazines had begun covering major events in the West, such as the Mexican War and the discovery of gold in California. They found a ready audience. These graphic stories and illustrations sparked the yearnings of Americans to abandon the safe confines of their civilized East and "Go West" in search of fortune and adventure.

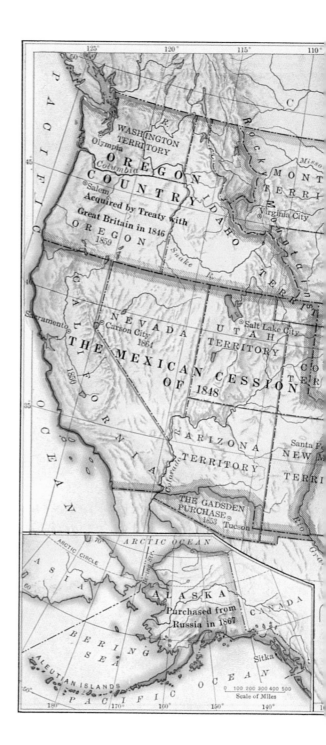

This map shows American expansion from the original coastal colonies westward into the new lands. Many of the expeditions into the West included painters and writers, whose journals and sketches recorded the landscapes and encounters with Native Americans. Stories from the trappers and Mountain Men, the photographers, artists, journalists, and writers who chronicled their travels and adventures—all were important sources of information on the Western territories.

From these written accounts and visual images, the region west of the Mississippi acquired a glamour that bore little resemblance to the rugged life of the frontier. For many Americans it was a wild chase to gold, free land and a life unconfined by government. It was this legend that fueled the nation, driving thousands of pioneers across the Great Plains and the Rocky Mountains to the Pacific Coast.

THE GROWTH
of the
UNITED STATES
From 1776 to 1867

The acquisitions made by the United States from 1776 to 1867 are shown by different colors.

The boundaries of the States and Territories at the close of 1867 are outlined by solid green lines:

The Capitals of the States and Territories in 1867 are shown on map by: ⊙

Scale of Miles

0   100   200   400   600

THE M.-N. WORKS.

A TIMELINE OF MAJOR EVENTS

PART I 1775–1861 *The Early Frontier*

UNITED STATES HISTORY

1776 Twelve of the thirteen states send delegates to Philadelphia where they draft the Declaration of Independence.
•The Continental Congress authorizes a flag for the United States. It will have thirteen stars and thirteen alternating red and white stripes.

1778 The Articles of Confederation are adopted by the Continental Congress.

1781 Congress ratifies the Articles of Confederation and Perpetual Union.

1783 The Revolutionary War ends when the U.S. and Britain sign the Treaty of Paris.

1787 Delegates from twelve of the thirteen states draft the U.S. Constitution.

1789 George Washington becomes the first president of the United States.

1791 The Bill of Rights is added to the Constitution.

1792 Thomas Jefferson forms the Republican Party to oppose the Federalists and to represent the rights of farmers and those in favor of a less centralized government.
•Washington and Adams are reelected president and vice president.

The first American flag

1796 Federalist John Adams is elected president and Democratic-Republican Thomas Jefferson is elected vice president.

1797 Adams is inaugurated as the the country's second president.

1798 Congress repeals all treaties with France and orders the U.S. Navy to capture French ships.

1799 Adams reopens negotiations with

THE LEGENDARY WILD WEST

1775 Frontiersman Daniel Boone blazes a 300-mile trail, known as the Wilderness Road, through the Cumberland Gap to Kentucky. He founds the town of Boonesborough on the Kentucky River.

1778 Jonathan Carver's book *Travels Through the Interior of North America* is published; it describes Indian customs and natural history of the Great Lakes and upper Mississippi regions.

Daniel Boone

1782 *Letters from an American Farmer* is published. The book contains impressions of America by J. Hector St. John de Crèvecoeur, who traveled through the Ohio Valley and Great Lakes region.

1784 Explorer and author John Filson publishes a map of Kentucky, based in part on surveys by Daniel Boone. He writes about Boone in his book *The Discovery, Settlement, and Present State of Kentucke.*

•Charles Willson Peale establishes a museum in Philadelphia; it contains many relics of Western Indian tribes, as well as plant and animal specimens collected in the West.

1785 Publication of an account of Captain James Cook's journey sparks public interest in the Pacific Northwest.

1799 Daniel Boone leaves Kentucky for Spanish land west of the Mississippi

France in an effort to avoid war.

1800 The presidential election results in a tie between Thomas Jefferson and Aaron Burr; the House of Representatives elects Jefferson president, and Burr vice president.
•The U.S. census cites the population at 5.3 million. Virginia is the most populous state.
•The Library of Congress is created.

1802 The U.S. Military Academy is established by Congress; it is located at West Point, New York, on the Hudson River.

1807 Congress prohibits slave trade with Africa, but illegal trade still exists.

1811 Construction begins on the Cumberland Road. It is the first major roadway project funded by the federal government.

1812 Congress declares war against Britain

Thomas Jefferson

on June 18. The U.S. is provoked by Britain's maritime policy in its war with France and by its relations with Indian tribes of the American Northwest.

1813 American forces achieve an important victory as they capture York (now Toronto). The retreating British destroy the fort rather than let it fall into the hands of the Americans.
•The Treaty of Ghent is signed on December 24, ending the War of 1812.

1818 The Convention of 1818 sets the border between the United States and Canada at the 49th parallel.

Illustration from Patrick Gass's journal

River, claiming that he needs "more elbow room."

1802 John Chapman, better known as Johnny Appleseed, begins planting apple trees in Licking County, Ohio. His planting eventually yields close to 100,000 square miles of fruit-bearing trees across the country.

1810 Zebulon Pike publishes *Expeditions to the Source of the Mississippi and Through the Western Part of Louisiana*, which describes his discovery of the peak that is named for him.

1811 Sergeant Patrick Gass, a member of Lewis and Clark's Corps of Discovery, publishes his account of the expedition.

1814 Jane Barnes, the first white woman to reach the Pacific Northwest, arrives at Fort George.

1817 Davy Crockett is appointed local magistrate in his home state of Tennessee.

1819 Chester Harding paints the only known representation of Daniel Boone from life, at Boone's homestead in St. Charles County, in the Missouri Territory.
•The *Texas Republican*, the first English language newspaper in Texas, begins publication.

UNITED STATES HISTORY

1820 The fourth census of the U.S. cites the nation's population at 10 million.

1821 The first public high school in the U.S. is established in Boston, Massachusetts.

1823 President Monroe presents his Monroe Doctrine to Congress. In it he warns European nations not to interfere in the affairs of countries in the Western Hemisphere.

James Monroe

1824 John Quincy Adams is elected president by the U.S. House of Representatives when none of the other candidates wins a majority vote in the national election.

1825 The Erie Canal is completed; it runs from Lake Erie to the Hudson River at Albany, New York.

1826 Thomas Jefferson and John Adams die on the same day—July 4, 1826.

1834 Abraham Lincoln enters politics for the first time, joining the assembly of the Illinois legislature.

He is twenty-five years old.

1835 The national debt is completely paid off as a result of revenues from increased railroad construction and skyrocketing land values.

1836 Abolitionists present anti-slavery petitions to Congress.

1837 Mount Holyoke, the first permanent women's college, is founded in Massachusetts.

THE LEGENDARY WILD WEST

1823 Major Stephen Long's journal, *Expedition From Pittsburgh to the Rocky Mountains,* is published.

1832 George Catlin begins an eight-year journey up the Missouri River into Indian country; he paints more than 600 views of Indian life and Western landscapes.

1833 German explorer and naturalist Prince Maximilian of Wied Nuwied travels up the Missouri River, accompanied by Swiss artist Carl Bodmer, who does a series of paintings on the customs of Plains Indian tribes.

1835 The first of Davy Crockett's *Almanacks* is published; it is filled with tales about Davy Crockett, who has become a popular symbol of the American frontier.

1836 Washington Irving publishes *Astoria,* recounting the earliest attempt to settle Oregon from 1811 to 1813.

1840 In his book *Two years Before the Mast,* Richard H. Dana describes his adventures at sea and on the California coast.

1842 John C. Frémont publishes his book, which describes the expedition with guide Kit Carson to the Pacific Ocean via the Oregon Trail.
•*Commerce of the Prairies* by Joseph Gregg is published.

It describes his efforts to find the best route from Independence, Missouri, to Sante Fe.
•Naval officer Charles Wilde's book *Narrative of the U.S. Exploring Expedition* describes the Pacific voyage that strengthened U.S. claims to the Oregon Territory.

1846 Francis Parkman travels west from Independence, Missouri, on the Oregon Trail. His experiences living with the Sioux

1840 William Henry Harrison defeats Martin Van Buren in the presidential elections, using the campaign slogan "Tippecanoe and Tyler, too." John Tyler is elected vice president.

1841 President Harrison dies after one month in office. John Tyler succeeds him as president.

1845 The House and the Senate adopt a joint resolution calling for the annexation of Texas. It becomes the twenty-eighth state in the Union.

1848 A coalition of antislavery groups forms the Free Soil Party and nominates Martin Van Buren for president.

1849 The Gold Rush begins as the first gold miners arrive in San Francisco aboard the ship *California*.

1852 *Uncle Tom's Cabin* by Harriet Beecher Stowe is published, arousing strong feelings against slavery.

1856 A proslavery group attacks Lawrence, Kansas, a center of the antislavery movement. One man is killed. In a bloody retaliation, abolitionist John Brown kills five proslavery men at Pottawotamie Creek. The term "Bleeding Kansas" becomes a commonly used name for the territory.

1860 Abraham Lincoln defeats Stephen Douglas in the presidential election; he gets very little support from the slave states.

1861 The U.S. Civil War begins when South Carolina's forces fire on Fort Sumter near Charleston and the Union commander quickly surrenders. Robert E. Lee resigns from the U.S. Army to fight for the Confederacy.

and talking to frontiersmen were published in the *Knickerbocker Magazine* and later as a book, *The California and Oregon Trail*.

1847 "Oh, Susannah," a song by Stephen Foster, is performed for the first time; the song will be carried West as a "Gold Rush song."

1851 The advice "Go West, young man, go West" first appears in an editorial by John L.

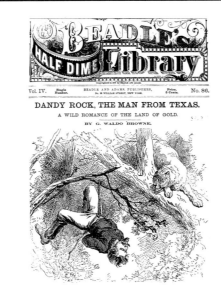

Title page from a book in Beadle's Half Dime Library series

Soule in the *Terre Haute Express*.

1855 *Frank Leslie's Illustrated News-*

paper, later *Leslie's Weekly*, begins publication, printing many stories and illustrations concerning the West. It is the first successful picture magazine.

1859 A play by F.H. Conroy, *Pike's Peak*, or *The Search for Riches*, opens in New York's Old Bowery Theater.

1860 *Maleska: The Indian Wife of the White Hunter*, the first of Beadle's Dime Novel Series, is published.

FIGHTING THE FRENCH AND INDIANS

The English colonists, who had settled along the Atlantic Coast, had been probing the Allegheny Mountains ever since John Smith sought river passages across the continent during the 1500s. From trappers and Indians, the colonists had learned of the wealth in game and minerals on the other side of the mountains. Tales of the bountiful Western frontier tempted many to leave the safety of the colonies and set out to discover the frontier for themselves. There were dangers there, however—particularly from hostile Indian tribes such as the Algonquins, who had sided with the French against the British and their colonial allies during the French and Indian War. Many frontier outposts had been attacked during the seven-year conflict, and the settlers were still at risk whenever they ventured beyond their settlements.

An attack in 1763 cost many colonists their lives. Pontiac, chief of the Ottawa Indians, had launched a rebellion against the colonists just as the French were surrendering to the British. But stories of frontier battles and of brave Western explorers only added to the notion that the West was an exciting new land, filled with danger and adventure. When the war finally ended, with the French losing almost all of their territories in North America, the exploration of the West continued at a rapid pace.

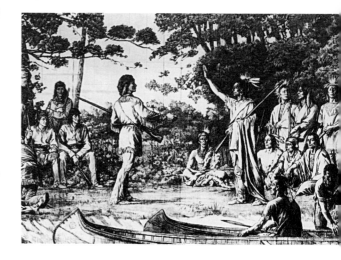

In this illustration (above), British Major Robert Rogers extends his hand to Ottawa chief Pontiac at the end of the French and Indian War. Artists often painted idyllic scenes of frontier life, depicting noble Indians, brave soldiers, and rugged frontier settlers. These early artistic impressions of the West helped to create a romantic vision of the American frontier.

One of the British commanders in the French and Indian War was Colonel Henry Bouquet. In this engraving (right), after a painting by American artist Benjamin West, Bouquet is shown negotiating with Pontiac's tribe at the British camp on the Muskingum River in Ohio in 1764.

THE LEGEND OF DANIEL BOONE

By the time of his death in 1820, Daniel Boone was known to millions of people around the world. Woodsman, Indian fighter, and pioneer, Boone was the subject of countless tales that helped make him a legendary figure of the early American frontier.

Born in Pennsylvania in 1734, Boone learned his wilderness skills at an early age and quickly became an expert hunter and trapper. He fought with the British during the French and Indian War and twelve years later led two explorations into the Kentucky wilderness. In 1775, he established a fort at the site of what later became Boonesborough. During the next two years, he gained a reputation as a fearless Indian fighter as he helped build and defend Boonesborough.

In 1784, the first published account of Boone's life appeared in John Filson's *Kentucke*. Boone became a symbol of American freedom and adventure. Although Boone was only fifty years old at the time, he was seen as an ageless frontiersman and an almost mythic figure. By this time, Boone was pursuing a career in politics, and he served as a legislator in both Kentucky and Virginia. This aspect of his career, however, received far less attention in the many books and stories that were devoted to his life. When Boone died in Missouri in 1820, he was firmly established as a frontier legend. Three years later, when Lord Byron wrote about Boone in *Don Juan*, Boone's name was famous throughout the world.

Daniel Boone is seen leading a band of settlers (the party that founded Boonesborough, Kentucky) through the Cumberland Gap in the Appalachian Mountains in 1775. Daniel Boone's exciting adventures became the source of countless stories and songs that helped to make Boone a frontier legend.

In this engraving based on a painting by C. Harding (left), Boone is pictured with a striking mane of white hair at age eighty-six, two years before his death in 1820.

This engraving (opposite) shows legendary frontiersman Simon Kenton rescuing Daniel Boone from a Shawnee Indian attack on April 24, 1777. Once out of danger, Boone reportedly thanked Kenton by saying, "Indeed you are a fine fellow." Kenton later gained renown as "the frontiersman too tough to kill." Captured by Indians in 1778, he was repeatedly forced to run the gauntlet and was tied to the stake three times. Kenton escaped, unassisted.

This illustration (left) by Charles Miller shows the fabled—but inaccurate—fate of John Stuart, friend of Daniel Boone. Stuart had been hunting in 1770 when he disappeared. The public immediately suspected he was killed by scalping, an Indian practice that was greatly feared at the time. Stuart's skeleton was located years later. The skull bore no sign of scalping.

MEN AND WOMEN OF THE FRONTIER

Pioneers living in the West, or traveling across the wild prairie, faced constant danger. The rough terrain, harsh weather, and the threat of Indian attacks made frontier life difficult for both men and women. Stories of brave pioneers and their incredible adventures were told in newspapers, magazines, and dime novels. Soon the exploits of these Western heroes and heroines were known all across the United States.

The sagas that described the pioneer's adventures were usually based on actual events, but details of the incidents were often exaggerated to make the stories more dramatic. Tales of battles in the wilderness, such as the siege of Boonesborough, were especially exciting. It was thrilling to read about the courageous men and women of that Kentucky settlement, lining the stockade walls and fighting off the hundreds of Indians who greatly outnumbered them. Other tales told of men engaging in fierce battles with Indians on the Plains—or of brave women, kidnapped by Indians, fighting to defend their children in isolated prairie cabins. These stories increased the mythic status of the Western pioneer.

As more and more people made the long journey westward, tales of their heroism spread across the country and around the world. An admiring public applauded the efforts of these determined pioneers who would stop at nothing in their relentless pursuit of a new life in the West.

At Boonesborough, battling hostile Shawnee forces led by Chief Black Fish, Boone and his men held out against the Indian warriors for almost two weeks, as shown in this illustration by Howard Pyle (above). The Indians were eventually forced to retreat after the tunnel they were building into the fort collapsed during a heavy rainstorm.

The heroic deeds of women, as well as men, made fascinating stories. One frontier heroine was Elizabeth Zane, seen here in this nineteenth-century lithograph by G. W. Fasel. When gunpowder ran low during an Indian siege of Fort Henry, Zane remembered a supply in her brother's house and braved the risk of capture to bring it to the defenders.

DOMESTIC MANNERS

OF

THE AMERICANS.

BY MRS. TROLLOPE.

" On me dit que pourvu que je ne parle ni de l'autorité, ni du culte, ni de la
politique, ni de la morale, ni des gens en place, ni de l'opéra, ni des autres
spectacles, ni de personne qui tienne à quelque chose, je puis tout imprimer
librement."—MARIAGE DE FIGARO.

VOLUME II.

LONDON:
PRINTED FOR WHITTAKER, TREACHER, & CO.
AVE-MARIA-LANE.

1832.

European travelers to America were the source of many of the books, articles, and illustrations of life on the Western frontier. In her 1838 book (left), Domestic Manners of the Americans, Mrs. Trollope described the rugged plantation life at Nashoba, in west Tennessee.

This lithograph (below) from Mrs. Trollope's book shows a worker surveying the partially cleared land, cabins, and outer buildings around the plantation at Nashoba.

CURRIER & IVES

Currier & Ives, a publishing company based in New York, produced over 7,000 lithographic prints dealing with a variety of aspects of American life, including the West, between 1852 and 1907. With their distinctive style depicting an innocent Victorian age, as well as a romantic vision of the West, the Currier & Ives prints helped create an enduring image of America in the late 1800s.

Founded in 1852 by Nathanial Currier and his brother-in-law, James Merritt Ives, the company competed for business with hundreds of other printmakers who were operating at the time in the United States. Currier & Ives, however, began to produce prints dealing with a wide variety of subjects— from fine art to illustrated journalism to scenes of the American West—and the public responded immediately, keeping the company highly successful for many years.

The firm employed a number of artists, including John Magee, Napoleon Sarony, and Louis Maurer. They produced scenes of Western landscapes, country life, sailing ships, and pioneers traveling across the frontier. While portraying realistic scenes, however, Currier & Ives prints were not necessarily true to life. A frontier landscape, "The Rocky Mountains," for example, was painted by an artist who had never even been to that part of the country. But Currier & Ives catered to the public's demand for sentimental and heroic pictures. Their prints created an illusion of a golden era of America with romantic images of the new West.

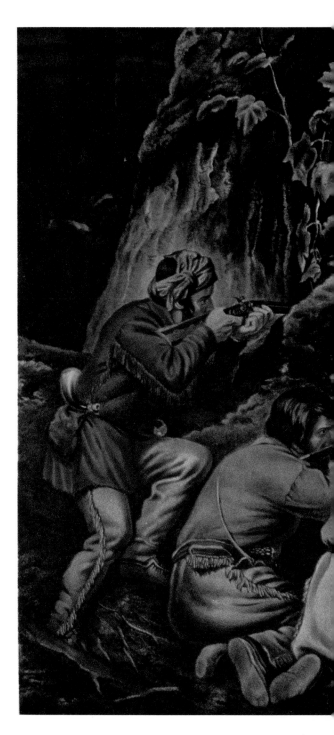

In 1834, Nathaniel Currier began publishing prints in New York for the homes of an expanding middle class. Popular subjects were presidents and military leaders, landscapes, and daily life. This print, titled "American Frontier Life," shows a skirmish between pioneers and Indians.

DAVY CROCKETT

Publishers in the East and in Europe were not the only sources of books, magazines, and popular prints about life in the backwoods. In 1835, a publisher in Nashville, Tennessee, began publishing *Davy Crockett's Almanack of Wild Sports in the West*, an annual collection of stories of the adventures of the famed frontiersman Colonel Davy Crockett.

Crockett, like Daniel Boone, is a figure about whom much has been written—some of it fact and some of it fiction. Born in 1786, he served as a scout for General Andrew Jackson in the Creek Indian War of 1813–14, and in 1827 he successfully ran for Congress where he served three terms. His greatest fame came in 1836, however, when he was killed at the Alamo in the Texas revolution against Mexico.

This cover of Davy Crockett's 1837 Almanack (right) shows Crockett dressed in buckskin, wearing a raccoon skin on his head, and holding his long rifle, nicknamed "Betsy." He became known as a symbol of the frontier, especially after his heroic death in 1836.

Illustrations and tales from the Almanack spoke of the brave deeds of other pioneers as well. This woodcut (below) shows a woman being attacked by a panther in northern Texas. According to the story, she reached her home just in time, where both her sister and her daughter shot the animal and saved her life.

Vol. I. "*Go Ahead!*" No. 3.

Davy Crockett's
18 ALMANACK, 37
OF WILD SPORTS IN THE WEST,
Life in the Backwoods, & Sketches of Texas.

O KENTUCKY! THE HUNTERS OF KENTUCKY!!!

Nashville, Tennessee. Published by the heirs of Col. Crockett.

THE CORPS OF DISCOVERY

The acquisition of the vast lands west of the Mississippi River in the 1803 Louisiana Purchase caused President Thomas Jefferson to push forward plans to explore and chart the region. He established a Corps of Discovery led by Captain Meriwether Lewis and Lieutenant William Clark to travel across the continent to the Pacific.

The expedition left St. Louis in the Missouri Territory in 1804, traveled up the Missouri River by boat, traversed the Rocky Mountains, and went down the Columbia River to the Oregon coast. The expedition had three basic goals: to help establish fur trade in the new lands for U.S. interests, to claim fertile farm lands for pioneering farmers, and to find a water passage to the Pacific.

Although a trained artist did not accompany the Lewis and Clark expedition, the historic findings were recorded in *History of the Expedition*, an official account published in 1814. Another book, *Journal of Voyages and Travel Under Lewis and Clark* by Sergeant Patrick Gass, who accompanied the explorers, was published in 1811.

Patrick Gass's account of the Lewis and Clark expedition (right), containing six engravings and geographical and explanatory notes, was published in 1811. The original report was drafted by Meriwether Lewis, who died in 1809.

This woodcut illustration (below) shows members of the expedition building a hut. The expedition wintered in 1804–05 in what is now North Dakota, and the following year in what is now Oregon, where they built Fort Clatsop.

Frontispiece. *Page 220.*

A Canoe striking on a Tree.

JOURNAL

OF THE

VOYAGES AND TRAVELS

OF

A CORPS OF DISCOVERY,

Under the command of Capt. Lewis and Capt. Clarke of the army of the United States,

FROM THE MOUTH OF THE RIVER MISSOURI THROUGH THE INTERIOR PARTS OF NORTH AMERICA TO THE PACIFIC OCEAN,

During the Years 1804, 1805, and 1806.

CONTAINING

An authentic relation of the most interesting transactions during the expedition; a description of the country; and an account of its inhabitants, soil, climate, curiosities, and vegetable and animal productions.

BY PATRICK GASS,

One of the persons employed in the expedition.

WITH GEOGRAPHICAL AND EXPLANATORY NOTES

THIRD EDITION—WITH SIX ENGRAVINGS.

[Copy-right secured according to Law.]

PRINTED FOR MATHEW CAREY,
NO. 122 MARKET STREET,
PHILADELPHIA.

1811.

Members of the Lewis and Clark expedition were fascinated and often startled by new species of wildlife they encountered. This engraving from Gass's Journal (left) shows an explorer who has been chased up a tree by a grizzly bear. The illustrator had probably never seen a grizzly bear before, and has drawn the animal somewhat inaccurately.

William Clark and others aim their rifles at a group of bears in this engraving (below), also from the Journal. The illustrator for the Gass book is unknown.

ZEBULON PIKE
AND THE
GREAT PLAINS

In 1805 and 1806, two important
explorations of the West were undertaken by Lieutenant Zebulon Montgomery Pike. His first expedition
searched for the source of the great
Mississippi River. During the expedition, Pike purchased land from the
Sioux Indians and established the first
U.S. fort in the Great Plains region—
Fort Snelling, in what is now Minnesota.

On Pike's second exploration the following year, his party explored part of
what are now Kansas, Nebraska, and
New Mexico. In Colorado he sighted
the famous mountain that would later
bear his name (Pikes Peak) in the
Rocky Mountains.

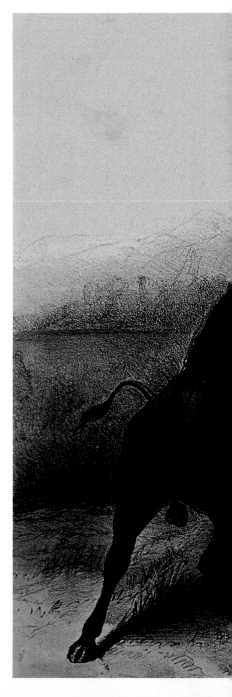

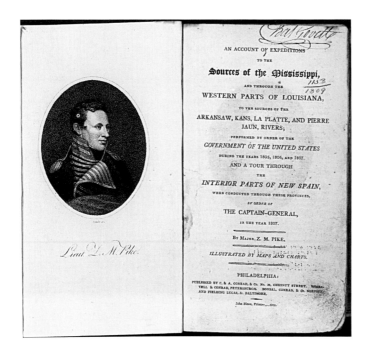

This portrait of Lieutenant Zebulon Montgomery Pike, after a painting by Charles Willson Peale, appears as the frontispiece to Pike's narrative of his journeys, An Account of Expeditions to the Sources of the Mississippi (opposite, bottom), published in 1810.

An enduring and popular image of the Great Plains, following Pike's expedition there, was the buffalo. These great animals would soon be nearly extinct, hunted out of existence as white settlers advanced into the West. This lithograph (below) by Currier & Ives is titled "The Battle of the Giants: Buffalo Bulls on the American Prairie."

PAINTERS AND SCIENTISTS GO WEST

In the early years of the nineteenth century, the United States government was sending military explorations to the West, but citizens in the East were equally interested in the wildlife and features of the new territories. In 1784 a leading painter and naturalist, Charles Willson Peale, established a museum in Philadelphia which contained Indian relics and plant and animal specimens, as well as his own work.

Peale had great interest in the natural history of the West. He encouraged his son, painter Titian Peale, to accompany Major Stephen Long's 1819 expedition up the Missouri River and across the Plains to the Rockies. Other scientists soon followed.

The title of this 1822 self-portrait of Charles Willson Peale (right) is "The Artist in his Museum." The bird and animal specimens were collected by the Long expedition and brought back to Peale's Museum.

This engraving (below) titled "Cavaniol Mountain" is from a book by Thomas Nuttall, a botanist who traveled to what is now Arkansas and Oklahoma in 1819.

Among Titian Peale's many studies of the West is this watercolor of a herd of deer moving across the prairie. Peale painted this picture, along with dozens of others of Indians and animals, while on an expedition with Major Stephen Long. Peale accompanied Long on two expeditions through the West—one in 1819, when they explored the South Platte River, and another in 1823 to explore Minnesota and Manitoba, Canada.

JOHN JAMES AUDUBON

John James Audubon (1785–1851) was the first widely acclaimed painter of the birds and animals of America. Born in 1785 in what is now Haiti, Audubon's first engravings were published in London between 1827 and 1838, in a collection titled *The Birds of America*. The book contained pictures of many birds native to North America and was the first study of its kind. Audubon based his engravings on birds which had been killed in the field to use as models for his work.

Audubon's second major work was *The Vivaparous Quadrupeds* (four-legged animals) *of North America*, an illustrated guide to animals in the wild. The collection, begun by Audubon, was completed by his sons after their father died in 1851.

This engraving (opposite) is from an oil portrait of John James Audubon, which was painted by an unknown artist in the nineteenth century. Shown in the wilds of Kentucky with his field binoculars and his hunting dog, Audubon was most at home in the woods and hills, studying birds and other kinds of wildlife in their natural habitats.

In 1826, when Audubon took the first of his bird drawings to Great Britain for publication, he was immediately recognized as a genius. His drawings, although occasionally lacking in scientific accuracy, were regarded as masterpieces. This engraving, called "Prairie Wolves," is from The Vivaparous Quadrupeds of North America.

GEORGE CATLIN

George Catlin (1796–1872), a native of Pennsylvania, became interested in the West while working as a young portrait artist in Philadelphia in the 1820s. One day, outside Charles Willson Peale's museum, he saw a group of Indian chieftains who had come to Philadelphia on their way to Washington to see "The Great Father"—the U.S. president. Catlin greatly admired the silent dignity of "these lords of the forest" and resolved to go West to "delineate the manners, customs, and character of an interesting people who are rapidly passing from the face of the earth."

In 1832, Catlin journeyed to St. Louis and then traveled by steamboat up the Missouri River to its junction with the Yellowstone River in what is now Montana. Many regard Catlin's paintings of the northern Plains tribes from this trip, and from the many other trips he made out West over the next ten years, to be some of the most important records ever made of Indian life in the nineteenth century. His work also stimulated concern for the plight of the Indians who were already being displaced from their lands. Following the passage of the Indian Removal Act in 1830, however, the Indians were forced even farther west.

Catlin's most famous book, Letters and Notes on the Manners, Customs, and Conditions of the North American Indians *(right), was published in 1841 in two volumes. The books, richly illustrated with Catlin's sketches, reflected his many travels throughout the West and are regarded as a reliable record of Indian life.*

Catlin showed himself in this painting (below), titled "Buffalo Chasing Back," riding a horse in the wild and rugged West. Catlin was known for his vivid portrayals of the Indian buffalo hunt.

LETTERS AND NOTES

ON THE

MANNERS, CUSTOMS, AND CONDITION

OF THE

NORTH AMERICAN INDIANS.

BY GEO. CATLIN.

WRITTEN DURING EIGHT YEARS' TRAVEL AMONGST THE WILDEST TRIBES OF
INDIANS IN NORTH AMERICA,
In 1832, 33, 34, 35, 36, 37, 38, and 39.

IN TWO VOLUMES,

WITH FOUR HUNDRED ILLUSTRATIONS, CAREFULLY ENGRAVED FROM HIS ORIGINAL PAINTINGS.

VOL. I.

NEW-YORK:

WILEY AND PUTNAM, 161 BROADWAY.

1841.

George Catlin's sketch (below) shows a rain-making ceremony as people of the Mandan tribe gather around their circular lodges to watch the ritual being performed. Catlin acquired a deep respect and affection for the Indians and their unique culture. The Indians grew to trust him, and allowed him to see aspects of their lives other whites never saw.

Catlin painted this portrait of the great Mandan chief Mah-Tu-Tuh-Pa, or "Four Bears" (right), in 1832. The chief's buffalo-skin robe is decorated with battle scenes and symbols of his bravery. Four Bears died, with most of the Mandan tribe, in a smallpox epidemic in 1837, only five years after Catlin visited the tribe.

In this drawing (below) by George Catlin, Native Americans engage in a traditional dance to invoke "the aid and protection of the Bear Spirit." The Pawnee Indians believed that the man who learned the nature of the bear would become like him—hard to kill, with the power of the sun.

CARL BODMER

Another important artist who visited the West in 1833–34 was Swiss painter Carl Bodmer, who accompanied the German adventurer and naturalist Prince Maximilian of Wied Nuwied. Together they traveled over 2,500 miles, including a long voyage aboard the steamship *Yellowstone* when they explored the Missouri River. During their travels they visited many Indian groups, including the Mandan, Hidatsa, Assiniboin, and Blackfoot tribes. Bodmer sketched over 400 scenes of Indian life, and later made paintings and engravings from the sketches. His watercolors were published in Maximilian's book *Travels in the Interiors of North America* between 1839 and 1843. The book revealed the strange landscape and the exotic people of the West and aroused even more the nation's growing excitement about the frontier.

This engraving, based on a painting by Carl Bodmer, shows Prince Maximilian and Bodmer meeting with members of the Minnetaree tribe. The illustration appeared in Maximilian's book, Travels in the Interior of North America, *published between 1839 and 1843. The prince's account of his daring trip, along with Bodmer's colorful paintings, established an early image of the frontier as a place of high adventure, filled with amazing sights.*

This painting by Carl Bodmer (below) shows Bellevue, Nebraska, located on the Missouri River south of Omaha. The oldest settlement in Nebraska, Bellevue was a trading post of the Missouri Fur Company from 1819 to 1823. It is said to have been named by the fur trader Manuel Lisa, who enjoyed the beautiful view of the Missouri River from the bluff.

This Bodmer facsimile of an Indian painting shows a Mandan chief and a Cheyenne chief engaged in fierce combat. The two tribes were bitter rivals but they were determined to fight fairly. After engaging each other with guns on horseback, both chiefs dismounted and fought with hand weapons—a tomahawk and a knife. Although the Cheyenne chief was more seriously wounded by the tomahawk, the Mandan let his enemy escape.

THE GOLD RUSH

On January 24, 1848, gold was discovered in the American River, a stream that flowed down from the Sierra Nevadas onto a ranch owned by Johann Sutter. Sutter's life, and his quiet, pastoral ranch in New Helvetia, California, would never be the same again.

Word of Sutter's discovery spread quickly as miners poured into California and began sending back pictures of the "golden land." Songs, dime novels, and tall tales about California's "mountains of gold" captured the imagination of Americans. Triumphant newspaper stories, such as those printed in Horace Greeley's *New York Daily Tribune*, added to the frenzy by urging everyone to pack up and "Go West." Thousands of people, dubbed the "forty-niners" by the enthusiastic press, began the long journey westward, hoping to get to California and find the next big strike. It was estimated that by 1860 over 260,000 people had made the overland trip in search of gold. Soon ships from all over the world set sail for the United States, as exaggerated stories of California's "instant millionaires" spread around the globe. Would-be prospectors from many countries poured into California, eager to join the Americans in their frantic search for the "mother lode." The land was changed forever.

In this comic look at Gold Rush fever, "The Way They Go To California" (opposite, top) reveals the desperate lengths some "forty-niners" would go to in their efforts to get out West and stake a claim. Whether they went on sailing ships, fantastic air ships, or just swam with picks and shovels on their backs, these hopeful prospectors were determined to use any means necessary to get to California in their scramble for gold.

A difficult part of the route to California was crossing the Sierra Nevadas. A party of emigrants is preparing to undertake this part of their journey in this illustration, which is the frontispiece to a book published in 1850, titled California: Its Past History, Its Present Position, Its Future Prospects.

Part II: 1862–1912
The Epic West

This lithograph was made in 1881 by Prang & Co., based on a painting by Thomas Moran called "Cliffs of the Upper Colorado River, Wyoming Territory." It is not clear if Moran actually saw a band of Indians preparing to ford the river, as depicted in the foreground. Renowned for his dramatic portrayal of the West, it is possible Moran introduced the Indians in this painting to romanticize the frontier.

In the West, veterans of the Civil War were leaving their shattered homes behind in search of opportunity on the frontier. There, a new war was being fought against the Indian tribes of the Great Plains with a devastating ferocity. Along with the war veterans, thousands of other Americans were making the journey west, encouraged by newspaper accounts, photographs, paintings, and stories of a land that seemed to offer endless possibilities.

Artists, too, continued their discovery of the West. Painters such as Thomas Moran, Albert Bierstadt, Frederic Remington, and Charles Russell created powerful images of a rugged landscape and people. Their impressions inspired scores of hopeful pioneers as they made the perilous journey westward.

The country entered the twentieth century under the leadership of Theodore Roosevelt, the "outdoor President," who was able to bridge the gap between the reality of the new frontier and America's romantic dream of the past. Roosevelt's affection for the Old West and its natural beauty made him a champion of conservationists such as John Muir, who encouraged the new president to preserve some of what was left of a West that was undergoing dramatic change. Under Roosevelt's dynamic leadership, the United States retained its frontier spirit while boldly entering a new, more modern, and uncertain world.

A TIMELINE OF MAJOR EVENTS

PART II 1862-1912 *The Epic West*

UNITED STATES HISTORY

1862 Two ironclad ships, the Union *Monitor* and the Confederate *Merrimack*, meet in the first sea battle of the Civil War, with neither ship winning a victory.

1863 Lincoln issues the Emancipation Proclamation, freeing all slaves in seceding states.
•Ulysses S. Grant and his Union troops defeat Confederate forces at Vicksburg, Mississippi.

1865 Lincoln is shot and killed by actor and Southern patriot John Wilkes Booth at Ford's Theatre in Washington, D.C. Vice President Andrew Johnson is sworn in as president.
•Lee surrenders to Grant at Appomattox Courthouse in Virginia, ending the Civil War.

1867 After efforts by Secretary of State William Henry Seward, Congress ratifies the treaty to purchase Alaska

The surrender of Lee to Grant at Appomattox

from Russia and appropriates $7.2 million for payment. The value of the territory is unrecognized and Alaska is nicknamed "Seward's Folly."

1869 Congress adopts the Fif-

teenth Amendment, which gives black men the right to vote in both the North and South.
•The Wyoming Territory passes the first law in the United States giving women the right to vote.

THE LEGENDARY WILD WEST

1863 Painter Albert Bierstadt goes to the Yosemite Valley to paint a series of landscapes that establish him as one of the master painters of the West.

1864 President Abraham Lincoln grants the Mariposa Grove of Big Trees and the Yosemite Valley to the state of California to be used as a state park.

Yosemite Valley

1867 At a salary of $500 per month, William Cody is hired by the Kansas-Pacific Railroad to kill buffalo that obstruct train travel. In eight months he slaughters more than 4,000 buffalo and becomes known as "Buffalo Bill."
•Photographer Timothy O'Sullivan joins Clarence King, a geologist with the U.S. Geological Service, on an exploration of the 40th parallel as the official photographer.

1871 William Bonney, better known as "Billy the Kid," commits his first murder at the age of twelve.

1872 Yellowstone becomes the first national park.
•*Mountaineering in the Sierra Nevada* by Clarence King is published.

1873 In their first train robbery, the gang of outlaws led by Frank and Jesse James derails and holds up the Rock Island Line train going from Adair to

1872 Congress creates Yellowstone Park in Wyoming to help conserve the nation's endangered natural resources.
•Congress adopts the Amnesty Act, allowing Southerners who had been involved in the Civil War to hold elective office again.

1875 Congress passes the Civil Rights Act, guaranteeing blacks equal rights in public places.
•Alexander Graham Bell and his assistant Thomas A.

Watson discover a method of transmitting sound across electrical wire. A year later, Bell will patent the first telephone.

1876 The National League of Baseball is organized. Boston beats Philadelphia in the first official game.

1878 The Democrats gain control of both houses of Congress for the first time since 1858.

1879 Congress passes an act

allowing women lawyers to argue before the Supreme Court.

1880 Wabash, Indiana, becomes the first town to be lit completely by electric light.

1881 Former school teacher and Civil War nurse Clara Barton organizes the American Red Cross.

1882 Overriding President Arthur's veto, Congress passes the Chinese Exclusion Act, pro-

hibiting Chinese laborers from entering the U.S. for ten years.
•Labor strikes by the Amalgamated Association of Iron and Steel Workers disrupt the railroad industry for several weeks.

1884 The Supreme Court declares it a federal offense to attempt to interfere with a person's right to vote. The case was brought by Southern blacks who had been prevented from voting by the Ku Klux Klan.

Advertisement for Buffalo Bill's Wild West show

Council Bluffs, Iowa. The engineer and a number of passengers are killed.
•Mark Twain's *Roughing It*, an account of his experiences on the Southwest and Far West frontiers, is published.

1876 The infamous mining boomtown of Deadwood is founded in the Dakota Territory; it is soon clogged with 7,000 miners who turn it into an example of frontier lawlessness.
•In attempting to carry out a bank

robbery in Northfield, Minnesota, five members of the James gang are ambushed by the alerted townspeople; only Jesse and Frank escape.
•"Wild Bill" Hickok, gold prospector and former marshal of Abilene, Kansas, is shot in the back while playing poker in Deadwood.

1881 In the mining town of Tombstone Arizona, marshal Virgil Earp, his brothers Wyatt and Morgan, and Doc Holliday, a dentist,

kill three men in a shoot-out at the O.K. Corral to cover up a stagecoach robbery.
•Billy the Kid is shot dead by Sheriff Pat Garrett in Fort Sumner, New Mexico Territory, having murdered twenty-one men.

1883 The first Wild West show by "Buffalo Bill" Cody is presented in North Platte, Nebraska.

A TIMELINE OF MAJOR EVENTS

PART II 1862–1912 *The Epic West*

UNITED STATES HISTORY

1885 The Washington Monument is dedicated in the nation's capital.

1886 The Statue of Liberty, a gift from the French, is dedicated in New York Harbor.

1888 Designer Phillip Pratt demonstrates the first electric automobile—a battery-powered three-wheeled vehicle.
•The worst blizzard ever recorded hits the Northeast, burying it under more than four feet of snow.

The Statue of Liberty

1890 The National Women's Suffrage Association forms in an effort to win women the right to vote in national elections.

1892 Annie Moore, an Irish immigrant, is the first person to enter the U.S. through Ellis Island.

1896 The Supreme Court rules in *Plessy* v. *Ferguson* that "separate but equal" facilities for blacks and whites are constitutional.

1898 The U.S. annexes Hawaii.
•The Treaty of Paris is signed, ending the Spanish-American War.

1901 President William McKinley is shot and killed by anarchist Leon Czolgosz at the Pan American Exhibition in Buffalo, New York. Theodore Roosevelt becomes president.

1903 Orville and Wilbur Wright

THE LEGENDARY WILD WEST

1887 Annie Oakley becomes the star attraction of Buffalo Bill's Wild West show, where she performs her sharpshooting tricks.
•Photographer John C. H. Grabill starts work on a photographic profile of the Dakota Territory, which he completes in 1891.

1888 Western artist Frederic Remington first gains public recognition with the publication of his work in a book by Theodore Roosevelt, titled *Ranch Life and Hunting Trails.*
•*Harper's* magazine publishes the first illustration by Charles M. Russell, who becomes known as the "Cowboy Artist."

1889 The first two volumes of Theodore Roosevelt's four-volume *Winning of the West* are published. The remaining volumes follow in 1894 and 1896.

1891 Yosemite State Park becomes a national park.

1892 John Muir is instrumental in founding the Sierra Club. Initially formed to fight the destruction of forests, its members later help create the National Park Service.

1893 Speaking before a Wisconsin historian's conference, Professor Fredrick J. Turner reads his famous essay, "The

A photograph of Deadwood by John Grabill

make the first successful airplane flight at Kitty Hawk, North Carolina.

1908 Automaker Henry Ford introduces the Model T, the first mass-produced auto in the world. Originally sold for $850, by 1926 the price is an affordable $310.

1909 Explorer Robert Peary reaches the North Pole.
•Black leader W. E. B. DuBois founds the National Association for the Advancement of Colored People (N.A.A.C.P.), a group that advocates intellectual and economic equality for blacks.

1912 The British ocean liner *Titanic* strikes an iceberg off the coast of Newfoundland and sinks on its maiden voyage, killing 1,500 on board, many of whom are Americans.

Orville Wright and his heavier-than-air flying machine

Significance of the Frontier in American History," which suggests that the presence of a frontier has been a major force in the development of democracy in America.

1894 *Death Valley in '49*, a saga of the ordeal of getting to the California gold country, is published by William Lewis Manly.

1903 "Calamity Jane" Cannary dies in South Dakota. A star of the Wild West shows of her time, she first appeared in Deadwood in the 1870s, dressed in men's clothing and boasting of her excellent marksmanship, her exploits as a Pony Express rider, and her stint as a scout in General Custer's forces.
•The first movie with a Western plot, *The Great Train Robbery*, dramatizes a story about the frontier.

1904 Zane Grey, a writer of stories about the West, publishes *Betty Zane*. His books sell by the millions.

1905 Theatrical producer David Belasco opens the first of a series of plays with Western themes—*The Girl of the Golden West*.

1907 *The North American Indian* begins publication. A monumental twenty-volume series written by Edward S. Curtis, with a foreword by Theodore Roosevelt, it contains more than 1,500 photographs of Indian life.

1909 Chiricahua Apache chief Geronimo, a great warrior and—in his later years—a rancher and celebrity at the St. Louis World's Fair, dies.

Geronimo

THE CIVIL WAR AND THE WEST

Although the great battles of the Civil War were fought in the East, the Western territories played a vital role during the war and were important to both North and South. The Confederacy was relying on important supply routes that ran through Texas and Mexico for badly needed food supplies and horses. The Southern forces also hoped to gain control over the valuable mining regions of Nevada and Colorado and then expand slavery into the West. The North was fighting to hold on to the rich mining areas that supplied essential resources for its war effort.

The Union victory at Vicksburg, in July 1863, cut off the South's supply routes to the West. This devastating setback, along with an earlier defeat at the Battle of Glorietta Pass near Colorado, ended the Confederacy's hope of controlling the Western territories. The North, after establishing control of the frontier, encouraged settlement of the territories in order to firmly establish federal authority in the area. The rapid development that followed changed the face of the West forever.

After the war, thousands of men from the Northern and Southern armies packed up their belongings and headed west, looking for work and adventure. Some would build railroads or work in the mines while others would become cowboys. Many of the ex-soldiers made use of the fighting skills they had learned during the war, and joined up with federal troops to help fight the Indian wars.

This engraving by George Bingham, "The Guerilla War in Bloody Kansas" (right), captures the anguish of a nation torn apart by the slavery issue. No longer isolated from the problems of the East, the Western frontier was dragged headfirst into the conflict. Here, after a brutal clash between pro- and antislavery groups, Brigadier General Thomas Ewing of the Union Army evicts Missouri settlers from counties along the Kansas border. Dramatic events such as this one focused the nation's attention on the West.

Frederic Remington's tough-minded vision of Western subjects such as Indians and the cavalry helped create the idealized impression that most Americans had of the West. In this painting, titled "The Cavalry Charge" (below), federal troops head into battle, riding at full gallop.

ART CAPTURES THE MOVE WESTWARD

Artists, already captivated by the American West, turned to the theme of westward expansion as more and more settlers made their way out across the mountains and prairies to start a new life on the frontier. Fascinated by these emigrants' grit and determination, as well as the drama of their journeys, artists such as William Ranney, Benjamin Rinehart, Emanuel Leutze, and John Gast all captured the heroic spirit of the pioneer.

American artists had long been waiting for recognition and were eager to emerge from the shadow of their European counterparts. The seemingly endless possibilities offered by the West gave them new opportunities and excited the imaginations of artists, their patrons, and ultimately the American public.

John Gast's "American Progress" (right), commissioned by publicist George Crofutt to promote a travel guide, shows trains, stage-coaches, and men trekking across the Great Plains on horseback and foot—all heading toward the new frontier. Floating above to guide the pioneers is an angelic woman in flowing robes; she is carrying a book of knowledge and stringing telegraph wires from the air. Farms, technology, and a new civilization follow closely behind.

In 1861, the United States government commissioned Emanuel Leutze's "Westward the Course of Empire Takes Its Way" (below) as a mural for the U.S. Capitol building. Leutze completed the mural in December 1862, and was paid $20,000. Critics and legislators alike were delighted with Leutze's painting of Mountain Men, pioneer families, horses, and mules—all struggling, yet triumphant—as they cross a mountainous Western landscape.

THE POPULAR PRESS AND DIME NOVELS

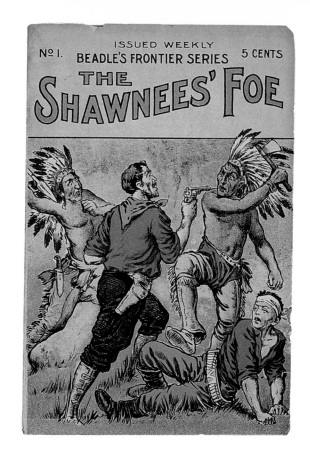

The public's fascination with the West was at its peak when Erastus Beadle, a publisher from Buffalo, New York, introduced the first dime novel in 1860. Filled with illustrations, the book told an exciting Western tale packed with action, cliffhangers, and daring rescues. Priced at only 10 cents, Beadle's book was an instant success. Encouraged by this first bestseller, Beadle went on to publish dozens of other dime novels that sold hundreds of thousands of copies.

Soon, other publishers were imitating Beadle's formula with equal success. Many of the dime novels were based on actual people and events— such as Billy the Kid and Wild Bill Hickock, and the deeds that made them famous. Much of what was written in these books, however, was pure fiction. The public couldn't get enough of these novels and sales were enormous. Western tales, along with detective stories and books about fictional heroes such as the daring Fred Fearnot, were bought all across the country. Most of the stories were wildly extravagant and helped contribute to the already exaggerated impression that people had of the West.

Books, magazines, and countless newspaper articles about cowboys, Indians, Mountain Men, and pioneers were published, adding to the growing collection of Western lore. Although the stories had little to do with the reality of the West, sales were brisk, as editors and publishers worked to delight an adventure-hungry public.

The popular press thrived on tales of action and adventure from the West. Dime novels such as The Shawnee's Foe (opposite, top) were a big hit with readers eager to experience Western excitement for themselves.

The press followed closely the exploits of William H. Bonney, known as "Billy the Kid" (left), until his death in 1881. In trouble since the age of twelve, when he dropped out of school (and supposedly shot his first victim), Billy led a life of robbery, gambling, and murder. His fame as an outlaw spread, and he was greatly admired by the public for his brash, youthful style and charming manners.

The law finally caught up with "The Kid" when he was shot to death on July 15, 1881, by his one-time friend, Sheriff Pat Garrett. The woodcut below is from Beadle's Half-Dime Library.

STAGECOACH BANDITS

The stagecoach was frequently the only means of transportation for both travelers and mail in the West, and it became a symbol of the adventurous life of the frontier. Tales of Indian attacks, robbers, and gamblers made the idea of riding the stage an exciting, if somewhat frightening, prospect. Many travelers were forced to make the trip, in spite of the fact that it could be a harrowing experience.

Robberies of the coaches were common. The open coaches were easy targets, and bandits knew that passengers traveling long distances were likely to be carrying money and valuables with them. Stagecoaches carrying mail and payrolls were also targets, and outlaws would acquaint themselves with a company's payday schedule and wait to ambush the stagecoach along the way. Even if passengers survived the trip without being robbed, they still had to endure rough roads and unpredictable weather. Despite the hazards, many stage lines operated successfully in the West.

The era of the stagecoach gradually came to an end and passed into American lore as tracks were laid across the country and the railroad became more popular. At right is a photograph of "The Last Deadwood Coach" by photographer John C. Grabill.

In "Robbing Wells Fargo" (opposite, bottom), robbers ambush a payroll coach as the drivers try helplessly to hold them off with whips.

Tales of stagecoach robberies made exciting reading. In this dime novel illustration titled "Robbery of the Express Car" (below), bandits chase down a stagecoach.

FRONTIER JUSTICE

Throughout the nineteenth century, many Americans living in the West settled their disputes violently, often relying on vigilante groups to bring law and order to the territories. Frontier violence, however, was not completely the fault of the settlers. The lack of judicial and legal agencies in the West contributed to the problem. When the pioneers moved west they settled in areas that had no courts of law or peace officers. This often made justice and protection matters of self-defense. The U.S. Army was the first organized agent of law and order on the frontier, besides the settlers themselves, and the military was frequently given the job of keeping the peace. Settlers began to appoint peace officers and judges for their towns, allowing them to collect fees and taxes as payment for their services. While bringing a semblance of order to the territories, this system also led to many corrupt officers and justices who would charge overly high taxes and fees in order to increase their salaries.

By the 1860s, towns and territories had begun to hire marshals and deputies to enforce the law. Lawmen like Wild Bill Hickock of Abilene, Kansas, and Bat Masterson and Wyatt Earp of Dodge City, Kansas, earned their reputations by keeping order in wild towns once known for their lawlessness. Appointments of peace officers and the establishment of law enforcement agencies gradually led to a more organized legal system in the West.

Frontier justice was often swift and unceremonious. "Execution of the Robbers" (above), shows a military firing squad carrying out the harsh sentence that was handed down to a band of thieves. The army was in charge of keeping the peace in frontier settlements when there was no marshal or peace officer in the territory.

This illustration (opposite, top) is titled "The Arrest of Bill White in a Crowded Saloon in Denver." Jail facilities in frontier towns were often poorly built and easy to escape from. Peace officers also had to contend with overcrowded cells and inadequate security at the jailhouse.

Courthouses were usually nonexistent in the Western territories. Trials might take place in a general store or saloon, as shown in this lithograph, "Trial of a Horse Thief" (right).

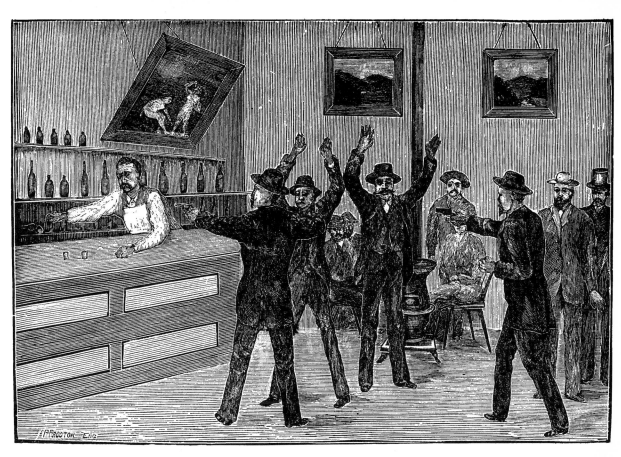

THOMAS MORAN

Thomas Moran was an Easterner, and his first exposure to the West was through a few rough sketches of Yellowstone he happened to see while working as an illustrator at *Scribner's* magazine in New York. Moran was so fascinated by Yellowstone's bubbling terrain and spouting geysers that he borrowed money so that he could accompany a geological expedition out West. Although he made do, grudgingly, with the minimum comforts of life in the rugged outdoors, Moran was overwhelmed by the beauty of Yellowstone and the West. He set to work immediately, recording the magnificent landscape that surrounded him.

When he returned to the East, Moran opened a studio in Newark, New Jersey, and turned out an astonishing number of drawings, watercolors, and lithographs based on his Yellowstone sketches. His work attracted immediate attention. One painting, "The Grand Canyon of the Yellowstone," was viewed by members of Congress, who were impressed. The painting helped convince them to create the nation's first national park at Yellowstone. Moran journeyed to the West four more times during his career and completed many landscapes of the West's wild and varied terrain.

Thomas Moran often made detailed sketches of the landscapes he intended to paint. Correct positioning and color of rocks, trees, and mountains were important to the artist. In this painting, titled *"Yellowstone Lake,"* Moran again reveals the startling beauty that inspired him to return to the West again and again.

ALBERT BIERSTADT

One of the most popular artists of the 1860s and 1870s, Albert Bierstadt was famous for his huge, romantic visions of the Western landscape. Bierstadt's larger-than-life paintings reflected the American public's grand perceptions of the West and helped create an enduring image of a frontier of mythic proportions.

Born in Germany in 1830, Bierstadt moved to the United States with his parents when he was two. In 1858, hearing of the amazing sights and mighty landscapes of the American frontier, Bierstadt made the first of several trips to the West to see the fabled land for himself. Sketching and painting as much as he could, Bierstadt returned to New England with drawings, paintings, and photographs. His paintings of the West were immediately popular. Working on huge canvases, Bierstadt painted oversized rocks and mountains and brilliantly colorful skies. His giant paintings commanded higher prices than those of any artist of the time. He was able to sell his work for as much as $25,000, an unheard-of sum in the 1860s.

By the late 1870s, Bierstadt's popularity declined. His once-expensive paintings were now being auctioned off for a fraction of their original price. Critics condemned his paintings as unrealistic and overly dramatic, while the New York art community regarded Bierstadt as self-serving and crude. He died in 1902, a forgotten artist.

Albert Bierstadt's dramatic, oversized paintings portrayed the West in deep, brilliant colors, showing huge rocks and trees, and mountains so tall that they seemed to disappear into the sky. It was this vast, expansive Western landscape that was popularized in the minds of Americans. This Bierstadt landscape, "Sunset, California Scenery," shows a lush sky over towering rocks and trees.

CAPTURING THE WEST IN PHOTOGRAPHS

The West was intriguing to artists because of its vast, unfamiliar terrain, its magnificent scenery, and the colorful and adventurous people who lived there. Painters had only to turn their heads to discover some new and wonderful scene waiting to be captured on canvas. Photographers, too, considered the West a dazzling subject, and they set out to record it with great enthusiasm.

Thousands of photographs of the West were taken in the 1800s, despite the cumbersome cameras and tripods that were used then. Hauling their equipment, photographers would hike up mountains, ride mules, and put themselves in the most precarious positions in order to get the picture they wanted.

Besides lugging around their heavy equipment, photographers had an additional hardship—they were dealing with a new invention. Taking a picture was not just a matter of clicking a shutter and developing the film. The cameras of the 1800s recorded their images on glass plates that had to be coated with a special chemical before being fitted into the camera. Then the photographer would make an educated guess about light exposure before positioning the camera at the proper angle. Once the plate was exposed, it had to be developed right away, usually in a darkroom-on-wheels, or in a "dark tent" set up by the photographer on the trail.

Determined photographers would go to any length to get the shot they wanted. In this photo by Carleton E. Watkins (above), taken in the 1850s, an unknown photographer perches on the edge of "Glacier Rock."

In another Watkins photograph from the 1850s, a lone tree stands before the massive rock formations of Yosemite (below). Watkins used an 18" x 22" plate in a giant camera that he built himself. His photographs of Yosemite earned him worldwide attention.

The towering walls of Canyon de Chelly are vividly captured in this photograph by Timothy O'Sullivan (left). While this image helped popularize the grandeur of the West, many Easterners were unaware of the Canyon's difficult history. In 1864, Kit Carson—following U.S. government orders—drove out the Navajo Indians, who made the canyon their home. During the "Long Walk" across New Mexico to a reservation at Bosque Redondo, almost 200 Indians died, and many others suffered from exposure and disease.

One of the earliest photographs to capture the magnificence of California's Yosemite Valley is this 1861 portrait by Carleton Watkins (below). The title, "Half Dome," refers to the sheer cliff seen in the background. This imposing granite wall would be memorialized by photographers for years to come.

THE NOBLE SAVAGE IMAGE

Following the Indian wars of the 1860s, much of the Indian way of life had been destroyed. Confined to reservations, and with many of their people dead from either war or disease, the Indians were no longer a threat to white settlements.

As the Indian threat diminished, America's perception of the Indian changed. The "primitive warrior," terrifying and fierce, was now being seen as a member of a doomed race, tamed by the white settler and "noble" in defeat. Earlier versions of this image of the "noble savage" had existed before the Indian wars, when the native people of North America were still being discovered by whites and were considered more a curiosity than a menace. Then, as the Indians fought to defend their lands against the white intruders' westward expansion, they were feared by whites once again as fierce enemies.

This attitude changed as tribes lost the struggle and were forced onto reservations. Whites were more likely to romanticize the Native Americans as simple creatures who were to be taken in hand and taught to live in a civilized world. Artists, too, helped to reinforce this image. Their appreciative public—happy, perhaps, to believe the Indian conquest a just one—was eager to applaud their efforts.

This portrait by E. S. Curtis of "The Wind Doctor" (above) shows a dignified Navajo medicine man. The medicine man was considered the spiritual leader of Native American tribes.

On some reservations, Indian children wore the clothing of their white peers when they attended school. In this picture (opposite, top), an Indian boy is escorted to class as others, in more traditional garb, watch his approach. In the background, a wagon adds another touch of the intruding white civilization.

The image of the "noble savage," and the idea that Indians had benefited from the white settlers' presence, became popular following the Indian wars. This American Bank Note Company engraving (right), shows an Indian at rest, peacefully watching the pioneers' inevitable progress across what was once his land.

THE WEST FOR SALE

By the late 1800s, images of cowboys, Indians, and buffalo were used to sell everything from books to clothing and food—even over-the-counter medicine. Politicians, too, recognized the popularity of the West and used it to their advantage when running for office. Even as early as 1827, Davy Crockett's fame as a frontiersman helped him get elected to Congress; his rugged outdoor image made him an attractive and highly recognizable candidate.

But perhaps the greatest salesman of the West was Buffalo Bill Cody. Performing with real heroes of the frontier, Cody staged Western scenes (based on incidents from his own life) in huge outdoor arenas in towns across America. Cowboys, Indians, and cavalry riders recreated famous battles and performed riding, roping, and shooting tricks.

Cody's show became world famous. Among its many attractions were cowboy stars like Buck Taylor and Annie Oakley, the "Little Sureshot." One year Chief Sitting Bull, who had defeated Custer at Little Bighorn, even toured with the show. Cody himself frequently reenacted his own famous scalping of Yellow Hand, a Cheyenne Indian, to the delight of the cheering crowd. "Buffalo Bill's Wild West" remained on the road for thirty years, touring and entertaining fans of the frontier.

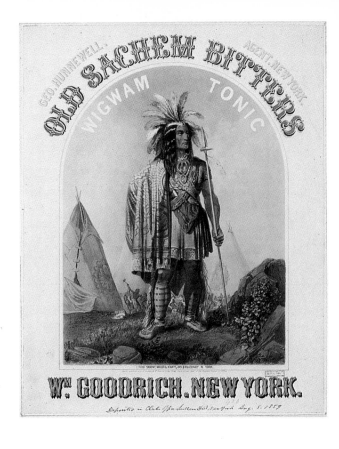

"Old Sachem Bitters" (above) uses a picture of an Indian in its advertisement for a "Wigwam Tonic." Indians were thought to use a variety of herbal folk remedies that were strange and intriguing to the public. This product identifies itself with the exotic image of Indian culture.

In the 1800s, anything Western was popular and attention-getting. A drawing of General Custer's battle to the death at Little Bighorn is used in this poster (right) to help sell a cure-all liver medicine.

FREDERIC REMINGTON

Frederic Remington was one of the most prolific and influential Western illustrators of the 1800s. Born and raised in the East, Remington spent years traveling across the frontier, working as a cowboy and riding with the U.S. Cavalry during the Indian Wars. All the while, he was sketching and painting, collecting images of the West and its people.

Remington was discovered by *Harper's Weekly*, which decided to use his painting of army scouts tracking Geronimo for the magazine's cover. Remington went on to have many of his drawings and paintings printed in magazines and books across the country. His realistic yet romantic portraits of cowboys and Indians, cavalrymen, and horses brought him worldwide recognition. Preferring to paint men and animals, Remington departed from many of the earlier Western artists, using the rugged landscape of the West as a background for the scenes of action and adventure he put on his canvases. Remington was also a sculptor who turned out a number of bronze figures dealing with the West. He was particularly proud of his ability to depict horses in motion, both in his sculptures and his paintings.

Although Remington continued to travel to the West, he made his permanent home in New Rochelle, New York, where he died in 1909.

Frederic Remington (above) completed over 2,700 paintings before his death on December 26, 1909. His work helped establish an enduring image of the West in the American consciousness. Although he depicted a romantic world of cowboys, Indians, and galloping ponies, his attention to detail and realistic portraits of even the most fantastic Western scenes lent credibility to his work.

The dangerous life of the frontier was a favorite Remington theme. In "A Surprise" (opposite, top), a terrified horse flees as two cowboys battle with an angry grizzly bear.

Remington's wood engraving, "Cowboys Coming to Town for Christmas" (right), presents a classic Western image: rough-and-tumble cowboys riding at a full gallop, whooping and hollering through a frontier town.

—FREDERIC REMINGTON
'89

Blacks in the West were rarely heard about, although many worked as cowboys and served in the U.S. Cavalry. Remington's engraving, "Captain Dodge's Colored Troopers to the Rescue" (right), illustrates an actual event: Captain Dodge, a black officer, and his men rescuing an outpost of white soldiers who were under attack by Ute Indians.

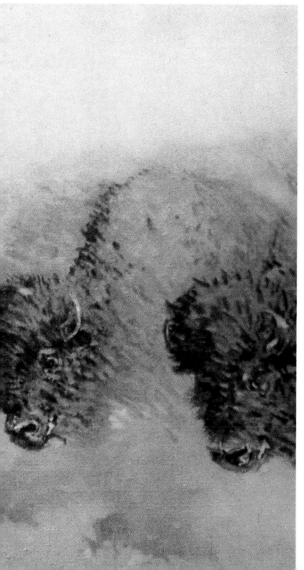

Many of Remington's illustrations were reproduced in Collier's magazine. "The Buffalo Hunter" (left) showed readers the dangers of hunting the huge animals. Accidents like this one were common, and hunters often risked their lives riding into a charging herd.

CHARLES RUSSELL, "COWBOY ARTIST"

Charles Marion Russell lived most of his life in Montana Territory and worked as a cowboy, trapper, and hunter for many years before he ever tried to make a living from anything as sedentary as art. Russell was born in St. Louis, Missouri, but he traveled west when he was fifteen and spent years working as a ranch hand and hunting in the mountains. During those years, despite a lack of formal training, Russell worked at his art. Always sketching or molding figures out of wax, Russell used his art to describe his experience in the West.

After working for eleven years as a cowboy, Russell decided to concentrate on painting and, if possible, make a living from it. At the age of twenty-nine he began painting seriously, but his embarrassment at charging for his work, and his tendency simply to give away most of his paintings, made the goal of becoming a self-sufficient artist more than a little difficult. Nevertheless, Russell's reputation as a "cowboy artist" grew. Russell was surprised to find that his paintings were soon commanding high prices and respect from a public attracted to the authentic quality of his art.

Russell's career lasted forty years. During that time he witnessed the death of the Old West that he loved, as towns grew into cities and the wild areas of his youth were tamed by growing development.

The realistic paintings of Charles Russell (left) that show a vanishing West earned him worldwide acclaim, but he had trouble taking money for his paintings. Russell, accustomed to getting no more than $25 for a picture, was astounded when one of his paintings sold for $6,000.

Russell spent years working and living in the West with both cowboys and Indians. In 1887, he lived in Canada for six months with the Blackfoot Indians, learning their language and customs. In "The Buffalo Hunt" (below), an Indian hunting party chases down a herd of charging buffalo.

THE STORIED WEST

When Owen Wister's novel *The Virginian* was published in 1902, there was a ready market for stories about the West. Dime novels, magazines, and cowboy poetry had been popular for years, starting in the 1800s. Many novels had been written about Indians, cowboys, and pioneers by authors as diverse as Mark Twain, Helen Hunt Jackson, and Washington Irving. Wister's novel, however, was something different. *The Virginian* told the love story of an Eastern school teacher and the brave, quiet cowboy she meets in the West. The novel was an instant bestseller as readers across the country responded to Wister's serious and realistic portrayal of life in the West.

Some of the earliest frontier literature had been written by James Fenimore Cooper, a New Yorker who had never been farther west than Detroit. His books told the story of an adventurous pioneer, Natty Bumpo, or Leatherstocking, who traveled with Indians across the frontier.

Early Western literature was usually divided into two categories: stories about the frontier and pioneer tales. Later, autobiographies of ranch hands and lively novels written by real cowboys, such as Charles Siringo, described life on the range and were immensely popular. Following the success of *The Virginian*, however, the formula changed. Now Western stories with strong, silent cowboys filled libraries and book stores and, later, movie and television screens.

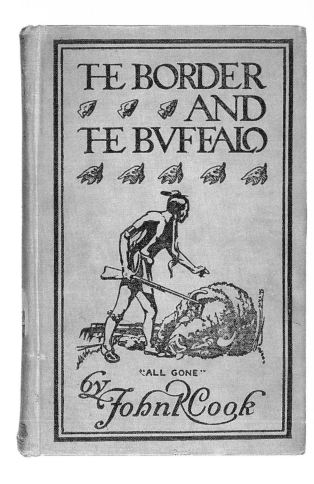

The Border and the Buffalo *(above) is a frontier tale of the vanishing West.*

The Virginian *(right) became a sensation almost overnight. By 1938 it had sold more than 1.5 million copies. It was made into a successful stage play and was later produced as a film four different times. In the 1960s, a television series based on the novel was a hit for years.*

Andy Adams's The Log of a Cowboy *(right)*, tells the story of a cattle drive from Texas to Kansas and is considered the best account of a trail drive ever written. Adams had worked for years as a cowboy in Texas until he was inspired to write his novel in 1903. The book was praised for its realistic portrayal of life on the trail.

Charles Siringo, author of A Texas Cow Boy *(below, right)*, was one of the first cattlemen to describe his adventures in the West. Born in Texas in 1855, Siringo worked for most of his life driving cattle herds to Kansas and New Mexico before he retired to write his popular life story.

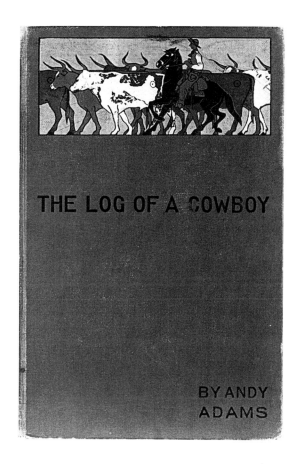

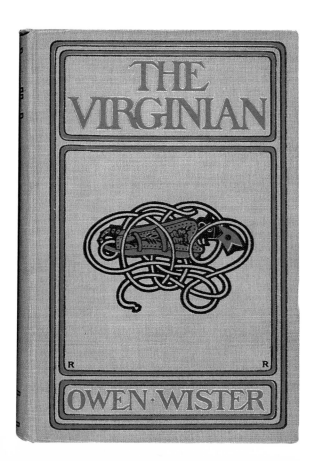

THEODORE ROOSEVELT

Theodore Roosevelt was a symbol of the frontier spirit. As president of the United States, he fought long and hard to preserve large areas of the Western frontier.

In 1883, at the age of twenty-five, Roosevelt left the political arena to head west and work at a ranch he had purchased in the Dakota Badlands. Arriving as a "tenderfoot," Roosevelt soon acquired the outdoor skills and the Western image that would serve him throughout his political career. Originally intending to stay out West for only a short time, Roosevelt remained for two years, riding and roping on his ranch. When Roosevelt returned to New York, he brought with him a love of the West and the great outdoors that would remain with him for the rest of his life.

In 1900, he was elected vice president on the McKinley ticket of the Republican Party. Six months after the election, Roosevelt, at forty-two, became the youngest president in American history, following McKinley's death from a gunshot wound. Roosevelt approached the presidency with the same vigor he applied to everything he did. Always loyal to his beloved West, he doubled the number of national parks in the country and made frequent trips to the now vanishing frontier.

This illustration (above) depicts Roosevelt killing his first grizzly bear on his hunting trip to the Bighorn Mountains. In his book about the trip, Roosevelt describes the bear as being "nine feet long" and weighing "over a thousand pounds."

A prolific writer, Roosevelt wrote a book about his experiences in the West. Ranch Life and the Hunting Trail *(left)*, published in 1885, describes his experiences bear-hunting in the Bighorn Mountains.

In 1903, when Roosevelt was president, he went on a camping trip in the Yosemite Valley with conservationist John Muir *(below)*. Impressed with the beauty of the area, Roosevelt became convinced of the need to preserve the many natural wonders of the United States. He later established Muir Woods, a natural preserve in Marin County, California, in honor of Muir's work on behalf of the environment.

THE WEST AS THEATER

Stories of the American West had delighted the public for many years. The drama of real-life Western adventures kept Americans, and people around the world, fascinated and intrigued. Cowboys, Indians, outlaws, and forty-niners were part of an incredible cast of characters set in a Western landscape that was spectacular in itself. With a public eager to experience the West firsthand, shows like "Buffalo Bill's Wild West" were wildly popular, recreating the drama of the frontier while creating a lasting and romantic image of the West.

As early as the 1830s, theater itself began using the frontier experience as American playwrights wrote about the heroic figures of the West. The play *Davy Crockett*, written in 1872 by Frank Murdock, glorified the great Tennessee frontiersman and ran for years in theaters across the country. Mark Twain co-wrote a play with Bret Harte about the Chinese experience in San Francisco called *Ah, Sin*, which was also a hit. But the most popular Western play ever written was an adaptation of Owen Wister's *The Virginian*. This stirring tale was already a huge success as a novel. Now the play gave audiences a chance to see their heroes in the flesh.

Western plays, and the enduring drama of an idealized American West, remained popular for years. With the advent of film and television, endless variations of the Western would be seen by millions for years to come.

Annie Oakley (above) performed for many years as part of "Buffalo Bill's Wild West." She amazed audiences with her shooting skills, performing daring, hair-raising tricks with a steady hand and a dead aim. Annie could shoot a dime from between her husband's fingers, and slice a playing card in half, edgewise, with a single shot.

This scene from a dramatic adaptation of Owen Wister's famous book, The Virginian, *shows the capture of "Steve" and "Spanish Ed" in Act III. These two characters were enemies of the heroic main character.*

BUFFALO BILL CODY

Perhaps the most famous figure to ride out of the frontier was William Frederick "Buffalo Bill" Cody. Hunter, scout, and Indian fighter, Cody personified the Old West and was one of America's greatest showmen.

Cody left his Iowa home at the age of thirteen and traveled west with a wagon train in search of adventure. Two years later he was carrying mail for the Pony Express, where he recorded the third fastest mail run in the company's history. Cody's familiarity with the frontier made him a valuable asset during the Civil War and he served as a scout for the Kansas Cavalry, which was fighting the Kiowa and Comanche Indians. After the war, Cody took up buffalo hunting and earned his famous nickname supplying meat to railroad workers in the West. He returned to scouting in 1869, joining the 5th Cavalry and gaining a reputation for being a fearless fighter in the Indian Wars.

By the 1870s, Cody's adventures and colorful nickname were making him the subject of newspaper accounts, dime novels, and at least one play (which he starred in, playing himself, in Chicago in 1872). Eventually, Cody started promoting himself, and in 1883 he created "Buffalo Bill's Wild West." Cody toured with the show for years and helped create an enduring and dramatic image of the American West. "Buffalo Bill" Cody died in Denver, Colorado, in 1917.

"Buffalo Bill's Wild West" attracted worldwide attention. In this portrait (above), Cody strikes a rugged pose during a performance at Olympia Stadium in London, where he successfully toured in 1903.

This lithograph from 1899 advertises "Buffalo Bill's Wild West and Congress of Rough Riders of the World: A Company of Wild West Cowboys." Cody was careful never to use the word "show" in any of the advertisements or literature about his performances. His aim was to recreate real-life scenes from the "Wild West," and he wanted the public to believe them.

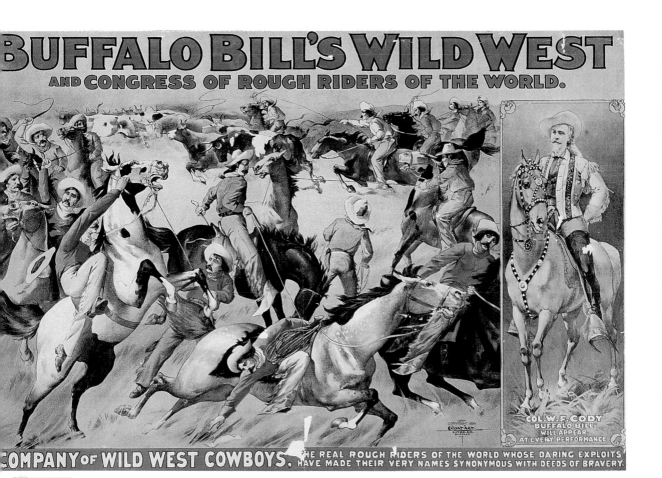

Resource Guide

Key to picture positions: (T) top, (C) center, (B) bottom; and in combinations: (TL) top left, (TC) top center, (TR) top right, (BL) bottom left, (BC) bottom center, (BR) bottom right.

Key to picture locations within the Library of Congress collections (and where available, photo negative numbers): P - Prints and Photographs; HABS - Historical American Buildings Survey (div. of Prints and Photographs); R - Rare Book Division; G - General Collections; MSS - Manuscript Division; G&M - Geography and Map Division.

PICTURES IN THIS VOLUME

2-3 Mountain, P 4-5 Poster, P, USZC2-3673 6-7 Indians, P

Part I: **8-9** Mountain lion, G **10-11** Map, G **12-13** TL, flag, G; BL, Boone, P, USZ62-1432; TR, Jefferson, G; BR, woodcut, P **14-15** TL, Monroe, G; BR, title page, P, USZ62-38980 **16-17** TL, Rogers, P, USZ62-42285; TR, Bouquet, P **18-19** C, Boone, P, USZ62-51136 **20-21** TL, Boone, P, USZ62-16240; BC, Stuart, P, USZ62-33991; TR, Kenton, G **22-23** TL, Boonesborough, R; BR, Zane, P, USZ62-2355 **24-25** TL, title page, R; BC, plantation, R **26-27** C, fighting, P **28-29** BC, panther, P, USZ62-50307; TR, title page, G **30-31** BC, building, P, USZ62-19230; TR, title page, R **32-33** TL, bear, P, USZ62-17371; BC, shooting, P, USZ62-19233 **34-35** BL, Pike, R; BC, buffaloes, P **36-37** BL, landscape, P, USZ62-11475; TR, Peale, R **38-39** C, deer, G **40-41** TL, Audubon, G; BR, foxes, G **42-43** BC, Catlin, G; TR, title page, MSS **44-45** TL, rain dance, G; BL, dance, P; TR, Four Bears, G **46-47** C, Minatarees, G **48-49** BL, Bellevue, P, USZ62-7780; TR, combat, G **50-51** BC, wagon train, P; TR, cartoon, R

Part II: **52-53** Cliffs, G **54-55** TL, surrender, G; BL, Yosemite, P; BR, ad, P **56-57** TL, statue, G; BL, Deadwood, P, USZ62-24378; TR, airplane, G; BR, Geronimo, P **58-59** BC, cavalry, G; TR, guerilla war, P, USZ62-808 **60-61** BC, Leutze, P, USA7-511; TR, Gast, P, USZ62-737 **62-63** TL, title page, G; BC, shooting, P, USZ62-38981; TR, Billy the Kid, G **64-65** BL, express car, P, USZ62-23788; TR, Deadwood coach, P, USZ62-5073; BR, Wells Fargo, G **66-67** TL, execution, P, USZ62-2157; TR, Bill White, P, USZ62-2100; BR, horse thief, P, USZ62-52108 **68-69** C, Tower Falls, G **70-71** C, sunset, G **72-73** TL, Watkins, P, USZ62-26579; TR, Yosemite, P, USZ62-17947 **74-75** TL, half dome, P, USZ62-56310; BR, Canyon de Chelly, P, USZ62-047670 **76-77** TL, Wind Doctor, P, USZ62-052476; TR, school, G; BR, hilltop, G **78-79** TL, ad, P; TR, Custer, P, USZ62-9203 **80-81** TL, Remington, P, USZ62-35031; TR, horse, P, USZ62-11320; BR, cowboys, P, USZ62-19223 **82-83** BC, hunt, G; TR, cavalry, G **84-85** TL, Russell, P, USZ62-43463; BC, hunt, G **86-87** TL, Border, R; BC, Virginian, R; TR, Log, R; BR, Texas, R **88-89** TL, bear, G; TR, title page, R; BR, Muir, P, USZ62-8672 **90-91** TL, Oakley, P, USZ62-7873; BR, Virginian, R **92-93** TL, Buffalo Bill, P, USZ62-22029; BR, ad, R

SUGGESTED READING

DANIEL, CLIFTON. *Chronicle of America.* New York: Prentice Hall, 1989.

JOSEPHY, ALVIN M., JR. *The World Almanac of the American West.* New York: Pharos Books, 1986.

MORRISON, SAMUEL E. *The Oxford History of the American People.* New York: Oxford University Press, 1965.

TIME-LIFE. *The Chroniclers.* New York: Time-Life Books, 1975.

Index

Page numbers in *italics* indicate illustrations